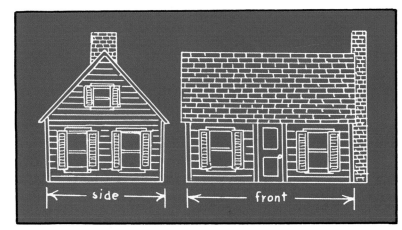

Building a House

by Byron Barton

Greenwillow Books, New York

Building a House. Copyright © 1981 by Byron Barton.
All rights reserved. Printed in the United States of
America. For information address HarperCollins
Publishers, 195 Broadway, New York, NY 10007.
www.harpercollinschildrens.com   First   Edition
ISBN 0-688-09356-6 (pbk.) 14 15 16 PC 10 9
Library of Congress Cataloging-in-Publication Data:
Barton, Byron. Building a house. "Greenwillow Books."
Summary: Briefly describes the steps in building a house.
1. House construction—Juvenile literature.   [1. House
construction.] I. Title. TH4811.5.B37690'.8373 80-22674
ISBN 0-688-80291-5   ISBN 0-688-84291-7 (lib. bdg.)
ISBN 0-688-09356-6 (pbk.)

On a green hill

a machine digs a big hole.

Builders hammer and saw.

A cement mixer pours cement.

Bricklayers lay large white blocks.

Carpenters come and make a wooden floor.

They put up walls.

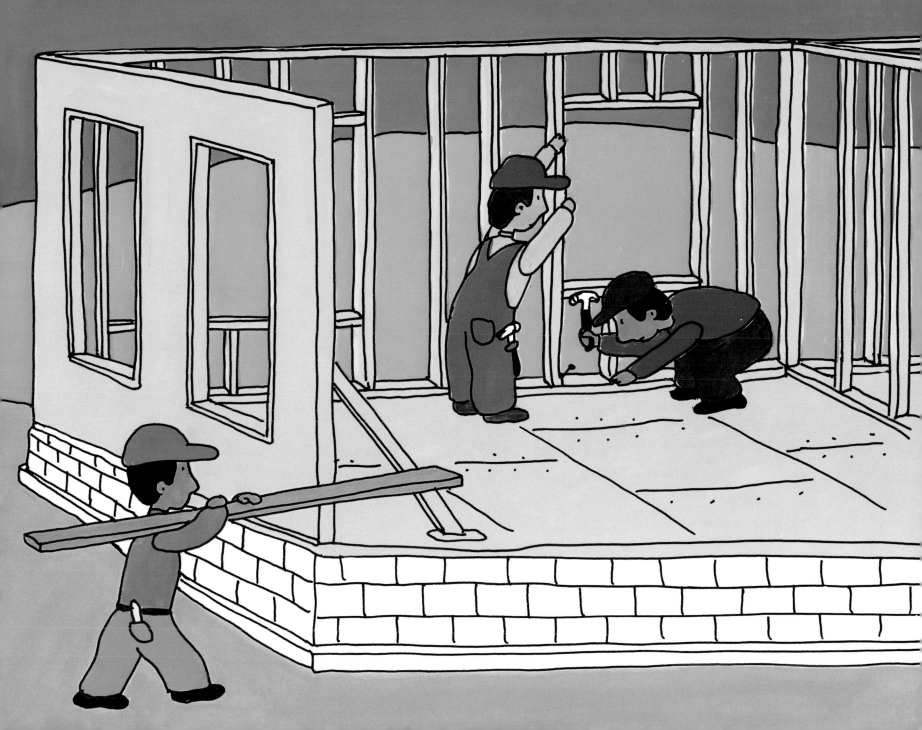

They build a roof.

A bricklayer builds a fireplace and a chimney too.

A plumber puts in pipes for water.

An electrician wires for electric lights.

Carpenters put in windows and doors.

Painters paint inside and out.

The workers leave.

The house is built.

The family moves inside.